BUILDING AMERICA

THE MILLS

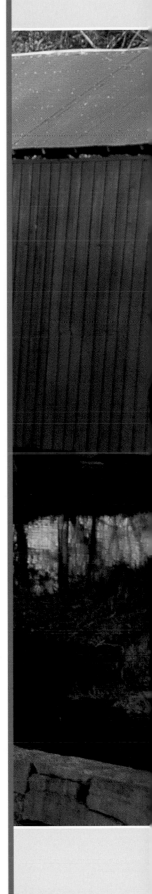

BUILDING AMERICA

THE MILLS

Raymond Bial

BENCHMARK BOOKS
MARSHALL CAVENDISH
NEW YORK

Benchmark Books
Marshall Cavendish
99 White Plains Road
Tarrytown, New York 10591-9001
Website: www.marshallcavendish.com

Library of Congress Cataloging-in-Publication Data
Bial, Raymond.
    The Mills / by Raymond Bial.
        p. cm. – (Building America)
    Includes bibliographical references and index.
    ISBN 0-7614-1333-2
      1. Windmills—History—Juvenile literature. 2. Water mills—History—Juvenile literature. [1. Mills and mill-work—History.] I. Title.

TJ823 .B48 2001
621.4'53—dc21

                                                                00-053019

Printed in Hong Kong
6 5 4 3 2

Photo Research by Candlepants Incorporated
Cover Photo: Raymond Bial

The photographs in this book are used by permission and through the courtesy of;
Raymond Bial: 2-3, 12, 18-19, 20, 22, 25, 26-27, 28, 30, 32-33, 36, 41, 43, 46-47, 50.
University of Virginia, Special Collections Department: 10. New York Public Library, General Research Division, Astor Lenox and Tilden Foundations: 11. Knights American Mechanical Dictionary, Boston 1876 ,figure 4627: 44. American Antiquarian Society: 13. Corbis: Lee Snider, 8-9; Wolfgang Kaehler, 6-7, 14-15; G.E. Kidder Smith, 17, 38-39. Courtesy of the Eric Sloane Estate: 16, 29, 34. Camden County Historical Society: 48-49.

Book design by Clair Moritz-Magnesio

CONTENTS

INTRODUCTION • 6

SAWMILLS • 8

WINDMILLS • 14

GRISTMILLS • 18

WATER MILLS • 26

MILLSTONES • 32

MILLERS • 38

MILL TOWNS • 46

GLOSSARY • 51

FURTHER INFORMATION • 53

BIBLIOGRAPHY • 53

INDEX • 55

A colonial windmill still churns near the historic town of Williamsburg, Virginia. Wind and water helped shape the lives of settlers in the New World.

INTRODUCTION

Long before steam and electric engines were invented, people operated mills wherever power from water or wind could ease the work of farming. Mills played a crucial role in the building of America. Both in the colonies and on the frontier, these little factories sawed logs into lumber and ground grain into flour. Windmills and water wheels moved gears to make barrel staves and ax handles and to turn pottery wheels.

Water spills from a sluice over the wheel of a restored sawmill in New Brunswick, Canada.

1

SAWMILLS

Settlers depended largely upon wood, just as for thousands of years, native peoples in the forested regions of North America had relied on trees as a source of fuel and a building material. In the colonies, people needed sawn lumber to build houses, barns, and outbuildings on their farms. In the villages that sprang up along the rivers and the Atlantic coast, they needed sawn lumber to build stores, workshops, schools, and churches. As settlers moved westward across the continent, log cabins dotted the landscape. However, whenever possible, people built houses from boards.

There were three ways to make boards, two of which were by hand. Pioneers rived, or split, logs with an ax and wedge—just as cedar is split to make shingles. However, these boards were rough and uneven. Or men laboriously sawed boards by hand. They laid the log over a trench about five feet deep and twelve feet long. One man stood in the pit under the log and the other stood over the log as they worked a long, two-handled ripsaw up and down. Both of these methods worked but were slow and exhausting.

So great was the need for boards that people turned to sawmills powered by water and occasionally by wind. In fact, sawmills were among the first structures built in the colonies. In 1623, not long after the founding of Jamestown (the first permanent English settlement in North

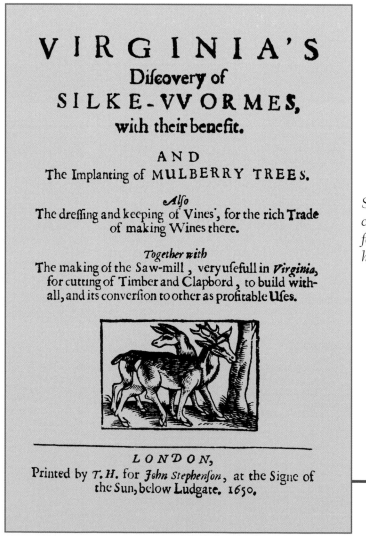

Sawmills in the American colonies turned out lumber for the construction of houses and other buildings.

A row of blades known as a gang saw, gears, and a waterwheel are depicted in this illustration from about 1650.

America), German craftsmen were brought to New England to construct a sawmill. One little sawmill could produce more boards in a single hour than could two sweat-soaked men sawing all day.

Since there were fewer rapid streams in the coastal South than in the North, fewer sawmills were built there. But in New England, nearly every town near a stream had a sawmill powered by a waterwheel, which together turned out hundreds of thousands of boards each year. The lumber was used not only in constructing houses, but also in a thriving ship-building industry. Because of the difficulty of moving heavy logs overland, mills had to be located near water, and there had to be lots of them. In Colonial America, sawmills seemed to be everywhere.

As the young nation expanded west, homesteads couldn't grow and villages couldn't prosper until a sawmill was built along a quick-flowing

A circular saw has been slicing massive timbers into boards in this sawmill since 1790 at Fort Mackinac, Michigan.

creek or river. Homesteaders floated logs downstream or dragged them to the mill with the help of sturdy oxen. Little more than a large open shed made of posts and beams with a plank sheathing, these frontier mills powered by a waterwheel housed basic saw machinery—sash saws simply moved up and down like large handsaws. In the early 1800s, several saws were grouped together at a mill, especially in regions where large numbers of people were settling. Later mills were fitted with circular saws, which left a unique mark on the lumber. Invented in England in 1814, the circular saw was not commonly used in the United States until the 1840s. It left crescent-shaped marks on the wood, while band saws, introduced in the 1880s, made closely-spaced vertical marks. Much later, scroll saws and jigsaws enabled mills to cut the elaborate gingerbread trim used on Victorian houses.

During milling, about a fifth of each log became sawdust. This sawdust often clogged and polluted the woodland streams. However, because the forests were so vast, people didn't worry about damaging them. At one time, it was said that a squirrel could journey, tree to tree, from the Atlantic coast to the Mississippi River without once touching the ground. However, the sprawling forests were quickly devastated by the sawmills until they were little more than a memory in much of the eastern half of the United States.

Sawmills helped the colonists to settle early America, but they were expensive to build and run. A skilled mason had to lay the stone foundation for the mill, and a carpenter had to make the wooden waterwheel. The foundation was especially important because of the constant shaking and vibration when the mill was in operation. A builder had to create a millpond to supply a steady flow of water. This meant constructing a retaining dam of earth, stone, or wood—and sometimes a combination of all three. He also had to fashion a wooden trough, known as a sluice, through which water flowed from the pond to the wheel.

Early American sawmills turned out huge amounts of lumber, as shown in this 1777 illustration of Fort Anne, New York.

Windmills with large, sweeping sails once dotted the banks of the Hudson River and the shores of Long Island.

2

WINDMILLS

Mills could be powered by wind, as well as by water. In 1633, in New Amsterdam (which became New York City), the Dutch constructed a windmill like those they had in the old country. Windmills were also erected along the barren shores of Long Island. Most pumped seawater into huge, shallow evaporating vats to collect salt, but a few ground flour or sawed logs into boards. In 1710, a traveler described his journey to New York: "As we sailed into the harbor the horizon was pierced by scores of windmills, taller than any we have seen elsewhere." Windmills became the basis of economic growth in New York.

Some early windmills were propelled by broad sails like those on ships of the era. Others relied on wooden stems sheathed with canvas. There is a nautical air about many of these early windmills, which were designed and built by sailors. Their operators were sometimes called dry-land sailors. Later windmills had wooden vanes with moveable louvers like in window shutters. The louvers could be adjusted to catch the most wind. The propellers on a windmill turned on a wooden beam called a whip.

Some windmills were stationary; they faced in the direction of the prevailing winds. However, most were either post-mills or smock mills that could be turned into the breeze. A post-mill was attached to a central post, and the entire building could be pivoted either by hand or by horse. In a smock mill, only the domed top of the mill turned. Some smock mills had a small wheel, called a flyer-fan, that turned when the wind came up and engaged a gear that moved the dome and its large propeller into the

The intricate wooden gears and propellers of a smock mill are depicted in these drawings by Eric Sloane.

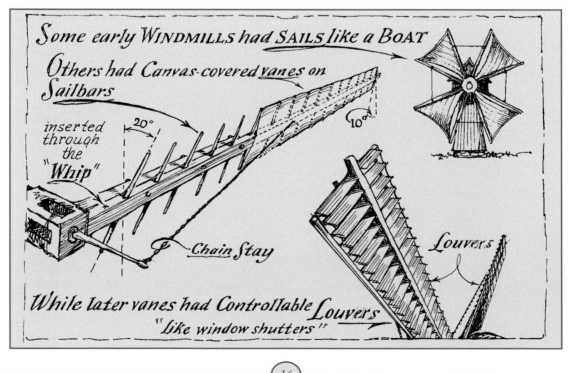

To operate a windmill such as this Rhode Island mill, the large propeller had to be turned to face into the prevailing wind.

wind. Smaller smock mills, called tower-and-tailpole mills, had a long pole fitted to the dome and a wagon wheel on the other end. By rolling the wagon wheel on the ground, two men could rotate the dome.

Windmillers had to be alert to the weather. No wind meant an idle mill, but if "caught with his sails up" in a storm, the miller was in serious trouble. The propellers churned so violently that the mill could be badly damaged and even wrecked. Sailors often looked to the direction of the Dutch windmills on Long Island and set their sails accordingly. Similarly, Long Island ferries could be counted on to be "operating daily, except when the windmills on the opposite shore have taken down their sails."

A long, high millrace carries water to the wheel of this stone gristmill built in southern Indiana in the early 1800s.

3

GRISTMILLS

Whether powered by wind or water, mills not only sawed logs into lumber but ground corn, wheat, rye, and other grains. People used many kinds of mills to grind grain into the flour or meal from which they baked bread. Native Americans used a hollowed log as a mortar and a long wooden post weighted at the top as a pestle. They placed corn into the hollow and pounded the grain until the hard kernels were broken down into coarse meal. Or they ground the corn by hand between two stones. In the early 1600s, settlers often used a

hollowed log and a wooden mallet to grind corn. Women often worked all day at this backbreaking work to grind just a few handfuls of cornmeal.

To ease their labors, settlers invented new grinding methods. By the middle of the seventeenth century, they had attached a log to a springy tree to make a sapling mill. By 1700, they had fashioned a plumping mill in which water was directed along a wooden trough into a scoop that filled and emptied rhythmically, causing a log to pound up and down like

Native American women ground corn with a mortar and pestle made from a hollowed log and a wooden pole.

Grain was poured down a wooden chute and through the damsel into the hopper. The hopper funneled the grain through a hole, called the eye, in the center of the top mill-stone, called the runner.

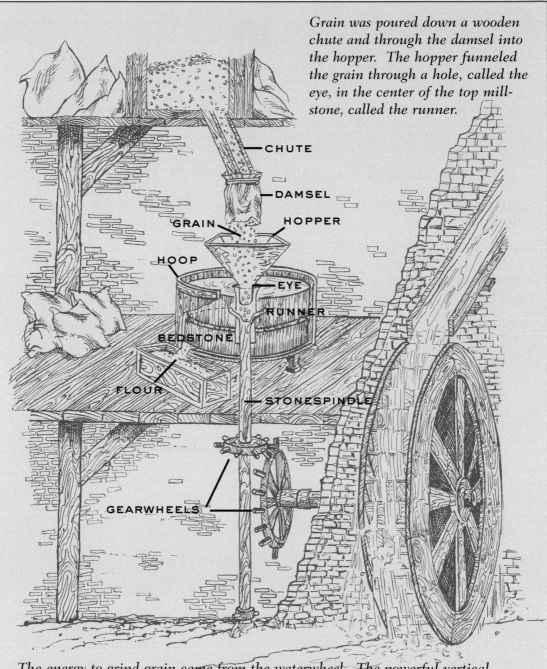

CHUTE

DAMSEL

GRAIN   HOPPER

HOOP

EYE

RUNNER

BEDSTONE

FLOUR

STONESPINDLE

GEARWHEELS

The energy to grind grain came from the waterwheel. The powerful vertical waterwheel turned a vertical gearwheel. This gearwheel meshed with a horizontal gearwheel, which spun the top millstone.

How a Gristmill Worked

Many gristmills, like this mill tucked away in the Great Smoky Mountains, were small but essential operations in frontier communities.

SMALL AND UNUSUAL MILLS

By 1800, people had devised a way to turn the quern by walking a harnessed horse or mule in circles. Horses also powered small mills to thresh grain, saw wood, and do other tasks on farms. Other unusual mills of the 1800s were dog mills, such as the Little Daisy in which a dog walked a treadmill to churn butter, and a turnspit in which a dog walked a wheel to rotate a fowl roasting in a fireplace. There was even an inclined merry-go-round mill on which horses tread to mill grain.

a wooden hammer. The sounds of distant plumping mills (also known as beating mills or sweep-and-mortar mills) carried across the forests and were often mistaken by travelers for Native American drums.

In the mid-1700s a pair of round millstones, one on top of the other, was employed as a quern, a simple, hand-turned mill. A man poured grain into a hole in the center of the top stone, which he then turned with a wooden handle. As the top stone rotated, the grain was crushed between the stones and then pushed to the edges to spill into a wooden barrel. The coarse flour that collected in the barrel gradually flowed down a spout into a wooden bucket.

As more people homesteaded on the frontier, they began to build gristmills to lighten their daily work. Grist means grain, and these grist-mills ground wheat, corn, and other grains for local homesteaders. Gristmills involved the same risks as sawmills, but they were more com-plicated and costly operations—both to set up and to run on an everyday basis. Millstones had to be imported from Europe and hauled to the mill site, often deep in the wilderness. A skilled craftsman had to set up and dress, or cut, grooves in the surface of the stone. When properly dressed, the two stones pressed against each other, crushing the kernels of grain and pushing the coarse meal or flour off the sides.

Settlers first had to find a good location for the gristmill—along a stream or near a waterfall—to power the machinery. The site also had to be near a forest, since a good supply of lumber was needed to build the mill. Some early mills were also constructed of stone. To ensure a flow of water all year long, people often made a millpond by building a dam across the stream. Sometimes, a miller sited and built a gristmill alone, but often everyone in the area came together to put up the mill, just as they helped each other raise cabins and barns. They squared heavy beams, often of tough oak, and pegged them together as the frame of the building. Then they sheathed the mill with clapboards or planks.

Millers often constructed a dam to manage the flow of water from the stream to their mill.

An overshot wheel sits near a quiet millpond.

4

WATER MILLS

Windmills were built in locations with little running water, as well as in a few early Dutch settlements. But most often people used water as a source of power. A number of different types of water mills were constructed, depending upon the geography of the river and the financial resources of the village or the miller. The most common types of waterwheels were the undershot wheel, the overshot wheel, the breast wheel, and the turbine. Undershot wheels were usually constructed near waterfalls along rapidly flowing streams. Water flowed under the wheel, turning its paddles at the speed of the current. These wheels could often be used year round, because the waterfall didn't freeze during the winter.

The overshot wheel required a millpond, a narrow canal known as a millrace, and a long, open wooden trough called a sluice to direct water over the wheel. Water from the millpond was channeled through the mill-race and into the sluice. The millrace allowed the miller to locate his mill some distance from the river—safely away from the threat of a flood that might wash away the building or weaken its stone foundation. When the

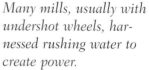

Many mills, usually with undershot wheels, harnessed rushing water to create power.

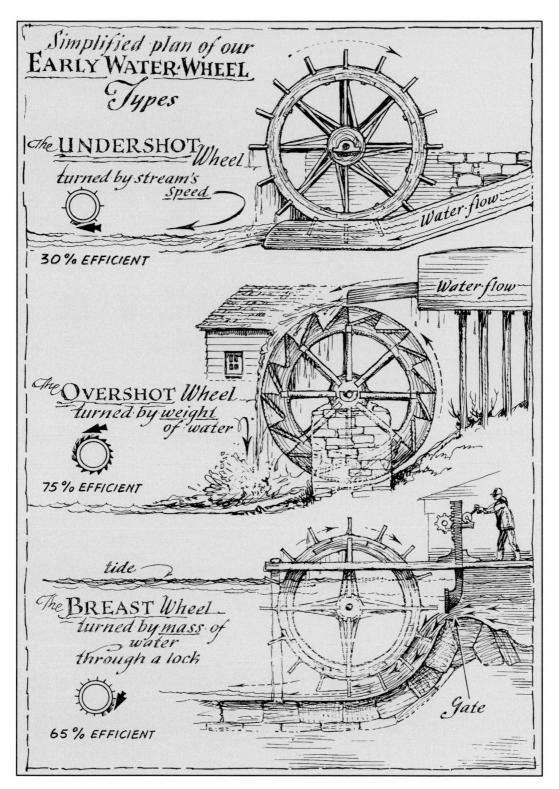

Three popular kinds of wheels and how the water flowed against them are shown in these illustrations by Eric Sloane.

A system of wooden gears transfers the immense power of the turning waterwheel to a pair of heavy grindstones.

sluice gate was opened, the water poured over a series of buckets, turning the wheel with its weight. The overshot design was the most efficient of all the water wheels. Even a little water could turn an overshot wheel because gravity and the weight of the water were enough to push the buckets downward, where they emptied and continued upward to be filled again.

In the breast wheel, or tide-wheel, water was also dammed in a pond and channeled to the wheel. But the water flowed against the middle of the wheel. The flow of the water was often controlled by a lock.

Placed underwater along a stream, a turbine could safely operate through the seasons, even if the surface of the river froze over.

Of all the wheel designs, the most common were the undershot and overshot, which were made in a thousand sizes and variations to fit the location and water flow at the mill site.

The turning waterwheel caused the whole mill to shudder and creak with tremendous energy. This power was captured and transferred through gears—only two gears in the most basic mill. The wooden teeth of these gears turned with each other and set the millstones in motion. A large vertical gear connected to the waterwheel and rotated slowly, turning a smaller, horizontal gear about a fourth of the size. Every time the larger gear made one complete turn, the smaller gear made four turns, thus concentrating the movement and spinning the millstone. To avoid sparks from the friction of the moving parts, which could ignite the grain dust and start a disastrous fire, the miller smeared animal fat on the wooden gears. Warmed by the turning, the grease lubricated the parts and kept the machinery running smoothly.

Craftsmen dressed millstones by chiseling grooves in circular or fanlike patterns on the surface of the stones.

5

MILLSTONES

The grooves on millstones were called furrows and the smooth surface was known as the land. The furrows were carved in many different patterns, all circular and fanlike. The two most common patterns were the sickle dress, in which the furrows curved slightly and came to a point at the center, and the quarter dress, which resembled a pinwheel. Millstones made from buhrstone were imported from France at great expense. Quarried in northern France, these stones contained a lot of silica and held their edge much longer than other stones. Since this buhrstone is found

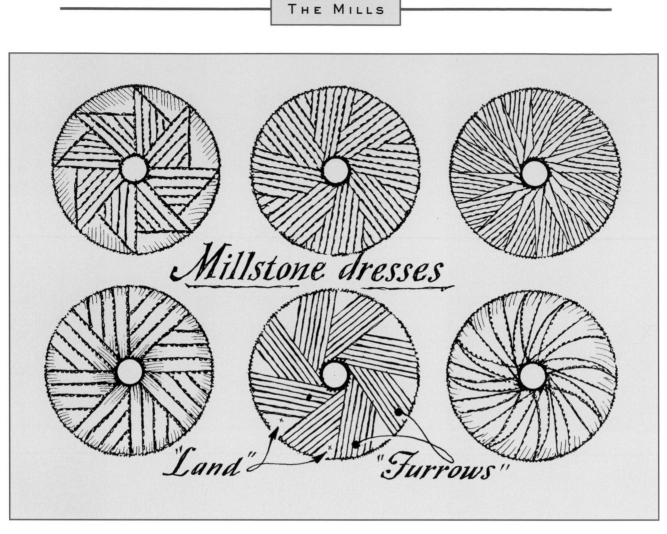

The most popular dresses for millstones are shown in this illustration by Eric Sloane.

only in small pieces, the stones had to be assembled in blocks, cemented together, and bound with iron bands. Millstones broke tough husks and shattered grains. Every few weeks, they wore down. The miller or a skilled artisan then dressed the furrows with iron picks. Sometimes bits of stone flew up and were embedded in the skin of the dresser's hands, which led to a popular saying, "to show his mettle," which meant to prove one's worth.

POPULAR SAYINGS FROM MILLS

Wait your "turn."

It's the same old grind.

Keep your nose to the grindstone.

It's just water over the dam.

He's been through the mill.

Milling around

Grist for the mill

Run of the mill

Just a cog in a wheel

Millstones worked in a pair known as a run. The bed stone was on the bottom, and the runner revolved over it. Attached to the runner was a spindle that went through the center hole and turned the stone. An iron bar kept the stones aligned as grain was poured into the center hole. Making sure the stones never touched, the miller set the distance according to the kind of grain to be ground. For example, corn needed slightly more space than wheat. The two stones were housed in a hoop. The meal or flour poured out of a little spout in the hoop into a wooden trough. From the turning of stones millers ground yellow cornmeal and white flour of exceptional flavor and texture. The friction of the two stones warmed the meal "like the underside of a settin' hen." Pioneers used the meal and flour to make bread, shortening bread, spoon bread, hush puppies, and cornmeal dumplings. Baked in a dutch oven, an iron pot with a lid, johnnycakes were a popular dish in many homesteads.

Mills became very complicated systems of gears, belts, chutes, and other interconnecting parts that conveyed the grain to the millstones.

The grain was fed into the millstones down a damsel, which was a chute with a cloth skirt, and into a hopper or storage bin. The hopper tapered to a small opening through which the grain poured onto the millstones. Sometimes, the flow of grain was controlled by a valve on the hopper. Turning about fifteen times a minute, millstones with different dresses made coarse or fine flour. Farmers often waited for mills to change to a favorite millstone before hauling in their grain. Later mills moved the flour by a spur-wheel drive along a conveyor belt. The meal then went into a dressing drum or cylinder of silk or screen in three textures to be sifted into bags of flour. The meal was also stored in the mill, usually on a dry upper floor, away from hungry rodents.

Two men fish the waters below a mill on the Mohawk River in New York, about 1854.

6

MILLERS

Early mills were often built by the millers themselves, but over the course of the nineteenth century, skilled carpenters and joiners became specialized craftsmen called millwrights. Here is an advertisement of a millwright from 1800:

JONATHON ELDREDGE
Hartford, Connecticut
Builder and joiner of sawmills, barley-mills, snuff-mills, corn-mills, tobacco-mills, mustard-mills, all made to be operated either by water or by horse.

Grist millers had to be highly skilled as carpenters, blacksmiths, and stone masons, as well as coopers and joiners to keep the machinery humming smoothly day after day, season after season. They learned to judge the character of the grain—its age, moisture, and temperature—and to set the proper speed for the rotating stone to ensure meal of the best texture. Good millers would rub a little flour between their thumb and fingers to judge the quality of the flour. Just by listening to the rumble of the gears, they could determine if the mill was working correctly. Hard workers, these men also had to be strong enough to lug heavy bags of grain and flour from early morning until late evening. People often said, "Remember the miller when you eat your daily bread." A single miller could handle the operation of a smoothly running mill. However, his children often helped by sweeping up, unloading wagons, and looking after the cats that stalked mice in the dark and dusty corners. And his wife brought meals to him and waited on customers during the busy harvest season.

Skilled millers were much in demand. Many came from Europe to operate mills at the edge of the wilderness. Many villages near streams tried to lure an experienced man, or "master," from another community by offering him a choice plot of land, as well as the mill and its site. He was granted a monopoly, which meant he faced no competition from other mills and was allowed a generous toll on every bushel ground into flour. Farmers had little or no cash, so the miller usually took a portion of the grain as payment. The first toll for grinding corn at Plymouth, Massachusetts, was set at four quarts for every bushel. In 1824, the Statutes of Connecticut permitted the miller to take three quarts for each bushel of grain; one quart for each bushel of malt; and one pint for each bushel of meal. Ten to fifteen percent of the grain to be ground was the average toll at most gristmills.

Early mills did other work in addition to sawing wood and grinding grain. Fulling mills were especially important. Before textile mills became

Millers sold their flour in cloth sacks decorated with colorful illustrations and gave it lively names, such as Queen Bee.

widespread in the nineteenth century, most settlers wore homespun. The newly woven cloth had to be taken to the fulling mill to be shrunk, washed, and brushed to give it strength and volume. The fuller, as the man who operated this type of mill was called, received the cloth woven in homes over the course of the year. He placed the cloth in long troughs of warm water called fulling stocks. Powered by a waterwheel, large oak hammers beat the cloth while the fuller added soap to complete the cleaning and processing. He then spread the cloth on racks called tenters. Edged with iron hooks called tenterhooks, this device kept the cloth from shrinking further. Finally, he raised the nap of the taut cloth by brushing it with teasel, a plant whose flowering heads have curved, rigid bracts. The fuller often placed racks of finished cloth in front of the mill to advertise the quality of his services.

In early America, most villages were widely scattered, so people were entirely dependent on the nearby mill for grinding their grain. Selling their extra flour, millers often became quite wealthy and respected. Many were elected to political office. Because of their privileged position, however, millers sometimes took advantage of the community. An old English saying, "No miller went to heaven," may be applied to at least some millers on the frontier. According to an old American saying, "The miller's hogs were always fat." However, in the United States, many villages had a time limit on contracts and so could get rid of a miller who charged too much or failed to do a good job grinding grain. The mill was like a public utility—the telephone and power companies of today—a business enterprise that made a profit but also served the common good.

From the late 1700s, millers relied on standard practices for the construction, maintenance, and successful operation of their gristmills. Books such as Oliver Evans' *The Young Mill-wright and Miller's Guide*, first published in 1795, were widely known and consulted. Cheerful and friendly, the best millers welcomed customers to the mill and charged them fairly. As a saying goes, "If it were not for the miller you would not have anything to eat."

The fuller at New Salem, Illinois—once the home of Abraham Lincoln—operated his mill within this substantial log building.

Among the prominent leaders in frontier villages the miller had the greatest practical importance. Usually the busiest man in the community, he both purchased grain and sold flour. He might also serve as banker and financial advisor to the people living in the village and the surrounding countryside. He was the first captain of industry in the young republic. Flour flowed to river and port towns in exchange for tools and household goods—pots and pans, axes and hoes, not to mention bolts of cloth and furniture—all because of the work he did.

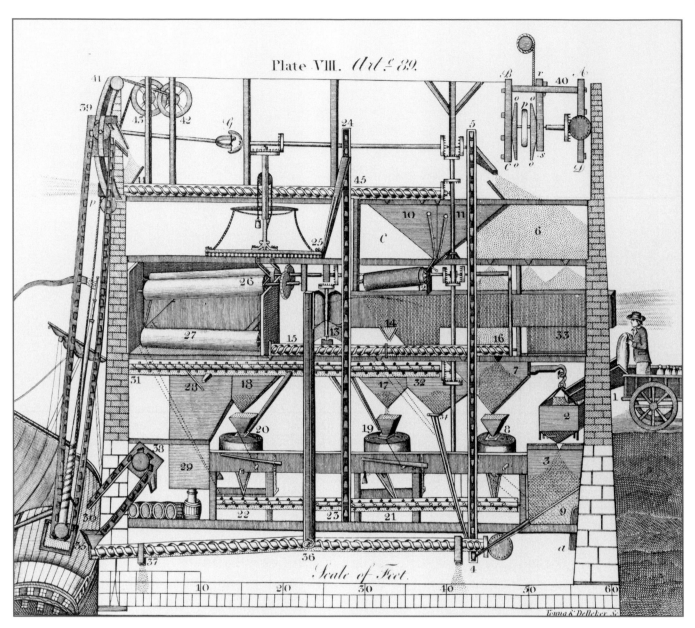

An illustration from The Young Mill-wright and Miller's Guide *shows just how complex the operation of a mill had become.*

The mill faced many hazards—mostly from the uncertainties of weather. A winter in which the stream froze might damage the waterwheel. Spring floods might burst the dam or even wash the mill away. A summer drought might dry up the streambed. High winds in any season might damage the blades of a windmill—or there might be no wind. Every mill had at least one working cat that kept the rats and mice from swarming over the grain and flour. Insects, such as moths, beetles, mites, and weevils, invaded the flour. Millers also worried about fire, since a single spark or the flickering flame of a candle could ignite the flour dust and send the mill up in flames.

Milling itself was also dangerous work. Millers often suffered accidents as they worked amid the whirling machinery. They could be struck by a windmill spar or caught and carried aloft on a whirling sail. Their limbs might be caught in the waterwheel or crushed in the gears. A common epitaph for a miller read, "Killed at his mill." Considered bad luck after a fatal accident, millstones were frequently used to mark the graves of the deceased miller.

This path through the forest leading to a secluded mill in the Appalachian Mountains is typical of those traveled by people long ago.

7

MILL TOWNS

Often journeying for days, even weeks, people had to first beat a footpath from their homesteads to the mill along streams with no roads, perhaps not even a trail. Yet they preferred stone-ground flour over the long hours of pounding corn and wheat by hand on their farms. They frequently waited to make the trip in winter when they could glide over the snow in horse-drawn sleighs or drive wagons over the frozen ground. If they lived on the other side of the stream, they had to find a suitable fording place for their wagons or construct a bridge to reach the mill. Over time, as roads became established, a village might grow up around the frontier mill—houses,

stores, workshops, schools, and churches. The village then became a gathering place for isolated homesteaders in the back country of America. According to a popular saying, "All roads lead to the mill."

Mills served as the wheels and gears of industry in the early years of growth and prosperity in the United States. During the first half of the nineteenth century, there were nearly one hundred thousand water-powered mills scattered across the nation. Quietly standing at the edge of a stream, mills symbolized the determination of settlers to make a home for themselves in the wilderness. Mills even figured in the settling of the West. In 1849, James W. Marshall discovered gold at a new sawmill—when he shut down the water on the millrace at Sutter's Mill in

By the mid-1800s, communities had sprung up around mills such as Haddon Mill, New Jersey.

California. "I reached my hand down and picked it up; it made my heart thump for I felt certain it was gold," he later explained. "Gold! Gold! Gold from the American River!" shouted Sam Brannon, waving a bottle of gold dust and spreading the word on the streets of San Francisco. "Forty-niners," as the prospectors came to be called, poured into California in the first of the great American gold rushes, which greatly spurred the growth of the West.

Throughout the United States, mills provided the necessities of life—shelter, food, and clothing. As men swung axes, felling trees in the forest, they relied on sawmills to turn their logs into useful boards. As farmers grew corn and wheat, they needed grist mills to grind the flour

that their wives baked into cakes and bread to feed their hungry families. Mills spun cloth and churned butter to ease the many chores around the household. Mills led to the development of new industries in the latter half of the nineteenth century. Today, many old winding roads lead to towns along swift rivers and streams where a mill once stood. Named after their mills, the many Milfords, Milltowns, and Millvilles of America are reminders of a time when these early "power plants" were at the heart of a bustling young nation.

Most mills have succumbed to progress, but some old mills still sit alongside streams and rivers.

beating mill   a general name for a small mill operated on a farm. Also called a sweep-and-mortar mill.

bed stone   in a pair of millstones, the bottom millstone that remained stationary while the top stone revolves. Also called netherstone.

breast wheel   a waterwheel in which water from a millpond is channeled against the middle of the wheel. Also called a tide-wheel.

buhrstone   a stone from France containing silica and used for millstones that grind the whitest flour and hold their edge longer than other stones. Sometimes spelled "burrstone."

damsel   a chute with a cloth skirt used to carry grain to millstones.

flyer-fan   a small wheel on a smock mill that turns when the wind comes up and engages a gear that moves the dome and larger propeller into the wind. Also called a flyer.

fulling mill   a mill in which cloth, especially wool, is washed, shrunk, and thickened. The man who operates this type of mill is called a fuller.

gristmill   a mill for grinding wheat, corn, and other grains. Grist means grain.

millrace   a narrow canal for channeling water into a sluice.

mortar   a hollowed log or bowlike stone in which grain is placed for grinding.

overshot wheel   a waterwheel in which water from a millpond is channeled through the millrace and into the sluice and over the wheel.

pestle   a long wooden post or a stone used for pounding grain. Used with a mortar.

plumping mill   a mill in which water is directed along a wooden trough into a scoop that as it fills and empties causes a log to pound up and down like a wooden hammer.

post-mill   a windmill in which the entire building is balanced and pivots on a central post by hand or horse.

pounder a hollowed log and wooden mallet used as a mortar and pestle to grind corn.

quern a pair of round millstones, one on top of the other, for grinding grain by hand and turned by means of a wooden handle.

rive to split a log with an ax and wedge.

run a pair of millstones working together.

runner in a pair of millstones, the stone that revolves and is on top of the bed stone (or netherstone).

sail a propeller, often sheathed with canvas, or moveable louvers like in window shutters, which turns on a windmill.

sapling mill a mill in which a springy tree is attached to a log. Often used for pounding corn.

sluice a long, open, wooden trough to direct water over the wheel.

smock mill a windmill on which only the dome above the mill turns.

spindle a wooden pole that runs through the center hole of the runner and turns the millstone.

tower-and-tailpole mill a small smock-mill with a long pole, one end of which is attached to the dome and the other to a wagon wheel. By rolling the wagon wheel on the ground, two men rotate the tower.

turbine a wheel placed underwater.

undershot wheel a waterwheel that rotates as water flows under the wheel and against the paddles.

whip a wooden beam to which the sails of a windmill are connected.

FURTHER INFORMATION

BOOKS FOR YOUNG READERS

Kalman, Bobbie. *The Gristmill*. New York: Crabtree Publishing, 1994.

Pernoud, Régine. *A Day with a Miller*. Minneapolis: Runestone Press, 1997.

Richardson, Adele. *Historic Mills*. Mankato, MN: Creative Education, 2000.

WEBSITES

Several of the following websites were consulted in the preparation of this book. The website for the Society for the Preservation of Old Mills is especially interesting and helpful.

Friends of Beckman Mill http://www1.minn.net/%7ehdunagan/
Hanford Mills Museum http://www.hanfordmills.org/
The History Channel Traveler http://www.historytravel.com/
Links to Other Related Mill Sites and Mill Sites
        http://www.angelfire.com/journal/millrestoration/links.html
National Parks Service Links to the Past http://www.cr.nps.gov/
National Register of Historic Places http://www.cr.nps.gov/nr/
Ohio's Old Mills Today http://fpw.isoc.net/KREK/
Pond Lily Mill Restorations http://home.earthlink.net/~alstallsmith/index.html
The Society for the Preservation of Old Mills http://www.spoom.org/
Water Mills of Yesteryear http://www.lanternroom.com/mills/millsel.htm

BIBLIOGRAPHY

Andrews, Ralph Warren. *This Was Sawmilling*. Atglen, PA: Schiffer Publ. Co., 1994.

Brownstone, Douglass L. *A Field Guide to America's History*. New York: Facts on File, 1984.

Dedrick, Benjamin William. *Practical Milling*. [Mishawaka, IN]: Manchester, TN: Society for the Preservation of Old Mills; Beaver Press, 1989.

Evans, Oliver. *The Young Mill-Wright and Miller's Guide*. Salem, NH: Ayer, 1989.

Fitz Steel Overshoot Water Wheels. Folkstone, CT.: Society for the Preservation of Old Mills, 1987.

Hopkins, Robert Thurston. *Old Watermills and Windmills*. Wakefield: EP Publishing, 1976.

Leffel, J., & Co. Leffel's *Construction of Mill Dams, and Bookwalter's Millwright and Mechanic*. Springfield, OH: J. Leffel & Co., 1881.

Leung, Felicity L. *Grist and Flour Mills in Ontario: From Millstones to Rollers, 1780s-1880s*. Ottawa: National Historic Parks and Sites Branch, Parks Canada, Environment Canada, 1981.

Magee, Henry. *The Miller in Eighteenth-Century Virginia: an Account of Mills & the Craft of Milling, as Well as a Description of the Windmill Near the Palace in Williamsburg*. Williamsburg, VA: Colonial Williamsburg, 1966.

Nordyke & Marmon Company (Indianapolis, Ind.). *Catalogue No. 48: Nordyke & Marmon Company, Flour Mill Engineers, Iron Founders and Machinists, Indianapolis, Indiana, U.S.A.* Knoxville, TN: Society for the Preservation of Old Mills, 1987.

Reynolds, John. *Windmills & Watermills*. New York: Praeger, 1970.

Sass, Jon A. *The Versatile Millstone Workhorse of Many Industries*. Knoxville, TN.: Society for the Preservation of Old Mills, 1984.

Sloane, Eric. *Our Vanishing Landscape*. New York: W. Funk, 1955.

Suggs, George G. *Water Mills of the Missouri Ozarks*. Norman: University of Oklahoma Press, 1990.

Water Power Equipment Manufactured by Fitz Water Wheel Co., Hanover, Penna. Folkstone, CT: Society for the Preservation of Old Mills, 1992.

INDEX

Page numbers in **boldface** *are illustrations*

accidents, 45
advertisement, 39
animals, 23, 45

beating mills, 23, 51
books, 42, **44**
breast wheels, **29**, 31, 51
buhrstone, 33–34, 51
butter, 23

Canada, **8–9**
cats, 45
chutes, **36**, 37, 51
cloth, 40–42, 43
construction, 13, 24, 39, 42, **44**.
    See also housing
contamination, 45
cooking, 23
corn, 19–20

dams, 13, 24, **25**, 45
dangers, 45
dry-land sailors, 16
Dutch, 15

ecology, 12–13
Evans, Oliver, 42

fire, 31, 45
flour, 37, 40, **41**, 42
flyer-fan, 16
fullers, 41, **42**, 51
fulling mills, 40–42, **43**, 51
fulling stocks, 42
furrows, **32–33**, 33, 34

gears, **16**, 16–17, **21**, **30**, 31, **36**,
    40
gold, 48–49
grain, 19–20, 35–37, **36**, 40, 42
gravity, 31
gristmills, **18–19, 21, 22**, 23–24,
    51

historic mills, **6–7, 12, 18–19,
    48–49, 50**
hopper, 37
housing, 9–11, **10**, **43**
    trim, 12
Hudson River, **14–15**

Indiana, **18–19**
insects, 45

Little Daisy, 23
locations, 11–12, 24, 27, 28, 31
logs
    as mortar, 19, **20**, 51
    as part of mill, 20–23, 52
    splitting, 10, 52
    transporting, 11–12
louvers, 16

merry-go-round mills, 23
Michigan, 12
millers, 16, 24, **38–39**, 40,
    42–45, 51
millpond, 13, 28, 31
millrace, **18–19**, 28, 51
millstones, 24, **30**, 31, **32–33**,
    33–36, **34**
millwrights, 39
mortar, 19, **20**, 51

Native Americans, 19, **20**
New Amsterdam. *See* New York
New England, 11
New Jersey, **48–49**
New York, **13, 14–15**, 15

overshot wheels, **26–27**, 28–31,
    29, 51
owners. *See* millers

payment, 40, 42
pestle, 19, **20**, 51
plumping mills, 23, 51
post-mills, 16, 51–52
pounder, 20–21, 52
power. *See* animals; waterwheels;
    windmills
products, 7, 10, 11, 23, 37,
    40–43, **41**, 49–50

querns, 23, 52

restorations, **8–9**
Rhode Island, **17**
riving, 10, 52
rodents, 45
run, 35, 52

runner, 35, 52

sails, 15–16, 52
sapling mills, 20–23, 52
sawmills, 9–13, **10, 11, 12**, 13, 23
saws, 10, 12
sayings, 34, 35, 40, 42–43
sea water, 15
settlers, 7, 9, 11–12, 20–23,
    47–50
shipbuilding, 11
sluice, **8–9**, 13, 28–31, 52
smock mills, **16**, 16–17, 52
Smoky Mountains, **22**
Southern United States, 11
standards, 42
streams, 11–12, 13, 27–28
Sutter's Mill, 48–49

tenterhooks, 42
tide-wheels. *See* breast wheels
tower-and-tailpole mill, 17, 52
towns, 47–48, **48–49**, 50
trade, 43–45
transportation, 11–12, **46–47**, 47
turbine, 31, 52

undershot wheels, 27–28, **28, 29**,
52
underwater, 31

Virginia, **6–7**, 10–11

wagon wheels, 17, 52
water, 11, 24. *See also* sea water;
underwater
waterfalls, 24, 27
waterwheels, 7, 12, **21**, 27–31,
    29, 42. *See also* breast wheels;
    overshot wheels; sluice; under
    shot wheels
weather, 17, 27–28, 31, 45
Websites, 53
whip, 16, 52
windmills, **6–7**, 7, **14–15**, 15–17,
    17, 45. *See also* post-mills; sails;
    smock mills; whip
wood, 9–12, 24. *See also* logs

Raymond Bial has published over fifty critically acclaimed books of non-fiction and fiction for children and adults. His photo essays for children include *Corn Belt Harvest, County Fair, Amish Home, Cajun Home, Frontier Home, Shaker Home, The Underground Railroad, Portrait of a Farm Family, With Needle and Thread: A Book About Quilts, Mist Over the Mountains: Appalachia and Its People, The Strength of These Arms: Life in the Slave Quarters, Where Lincoln Walked, One-Room School, A Handful of Dirt,* and *Ghost Towns of the American West.*

He has written Lifeways, a series published by Marshall Cavendish about Native Americans, traveling to tribal cultural centers, to photograph people, places, and objects that reflect the rich history and social life of Indian peoples.

Building America is the author's second series with Marshall Cavendish. As with his other work, Bial's love of social and cultural history and his deep feeling for his subjects is evident in both the text and the illustrations.

A full-time librarian at a small college in Champaign, Illinois, he lives with his wife and three children in nearby Urbana.